Sahara Survival

Written by Stephen Davies

Illustrated by Hatem Aly

RISING STARS

"I want to sit in the front seat!" shouted Ali, hurrying across the runway towards the little plane. "Please, Dad! May I?"

Karim smiled. "All right, son. You sit with me until we reach the town of Agadez, and then Amira can have a turn."

Karim's job was delivering brand new planes to rich people. He loved his work, and he was looking forward to flying with his children for the first time.

The children climbed into the shiny plane and put their seat belts on. Their father sat in the pilot's seat and laid a map of Africa on Ali's knees.

"This is Tunis, where we live," Karim said, pointing to a city on the map. "And down here is Lagos, where we'll deliver the plane."

The plane took off smoothly. It flew over the city and the countryside, and on into the desert.

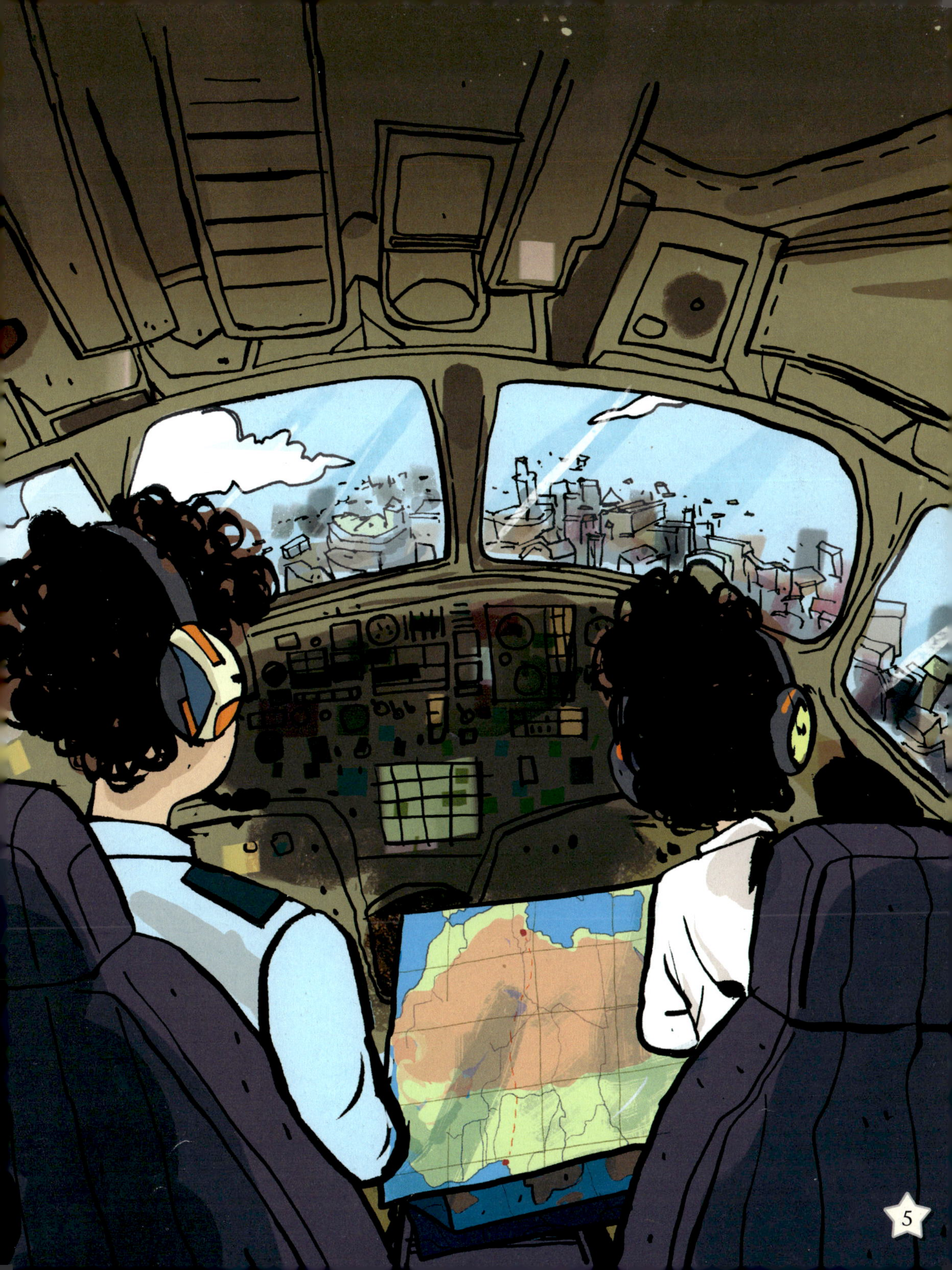

"We are nearing Agadez," said Karim. "We need to land there and put more fuel in the plane."

As the plane descended, it started to shudder and shake. The sky outside the windows went dark. A red light in front of Karim began to flash.

"I'm scared, Dad!" shouted Amira. "What's going on?"

"Sandstorm," replied Karim. "I can't see anything. We'll have to land in the desert."

Ali and Amira bent forward and put their hands over their heads. In the darkness, they could feel the plane getting lower and lower. It landed on the sand with a heavy thud.

"Aaaaargh!" they yelled.

"Ali! Amira!" cried Karim. "Are you okay?"

"We're fine," they replied. "What about you, Dad?"

"My ankle hurts. I think it's sprained."

The plane slid along the sand and stopped.

When the sandstorm passed, they climbed down onto the hot sand and looked at the plane. One wing was damaged and the wheels were broken.

"No more flying today," sighed Amira.

Karim looked at his phone. "No signal," he said. "We'll have to try and walk to Agadez."

"Which way is that?" asked Ali.

They gazed around them at the desert. The dunes all looked the same.

"I'm not sure," said Karim. "We're lost."

They sat under the nose of the plane and drank water from plastic bottles.

Amira fetched her suitcase from the plane. She took out her orange dress and Ali's white shirt, and started to rip them up.

"I'm making three turbans," she said, "and a bandage for Dad's ankle."

Ali found a long camel bone on the sand nearby. "This will make a good crutch," he grinned.

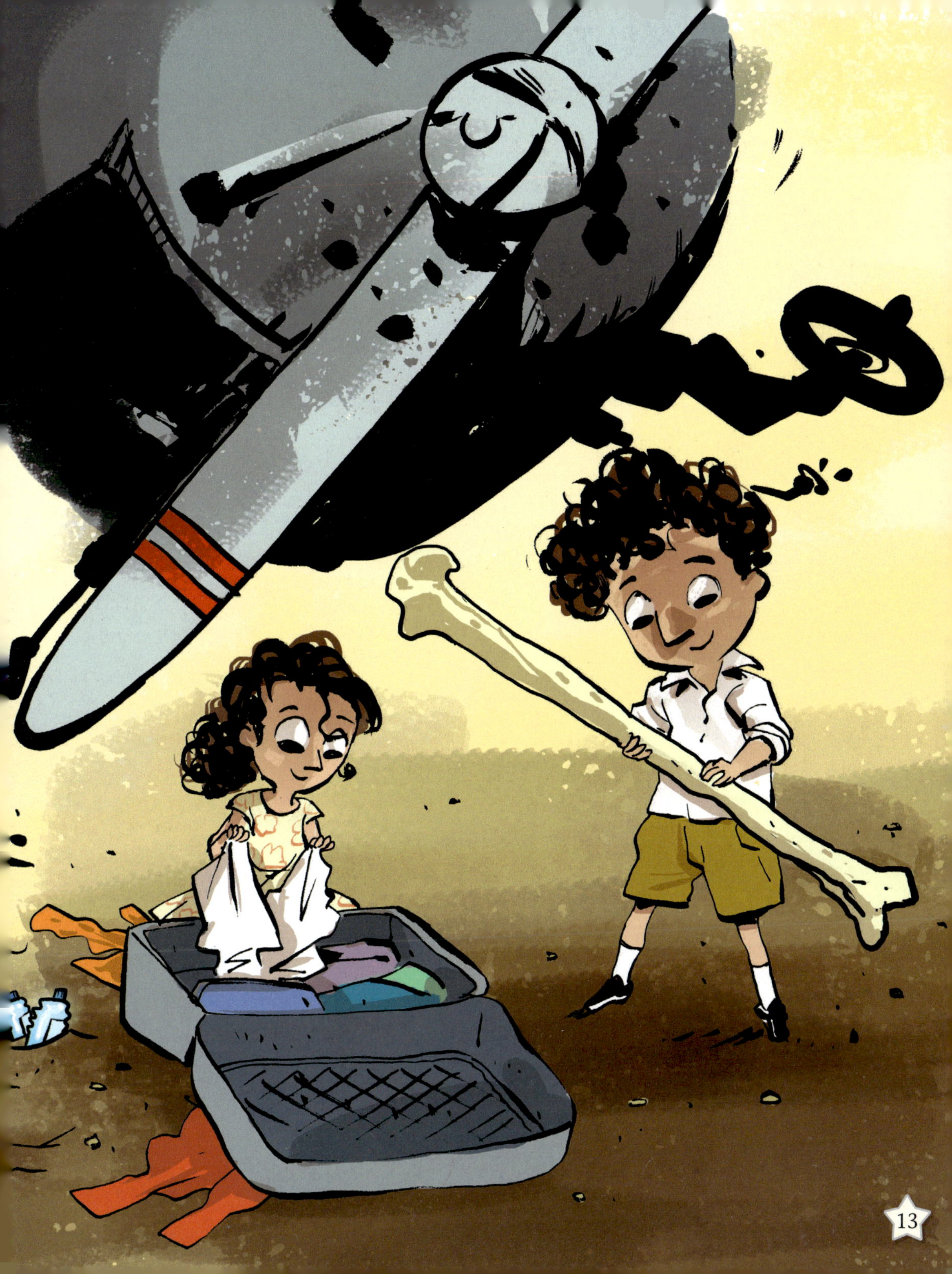

As the afternoon slowly passed, the sun dipped lower in the sky.

"We were travelling south when we crashed," said Karim. "We know that the sun sets in the west, so …"

"So Agadez is this way!" pointed Ali, starting to walk. "Come on!"

The family trudged among the dunes. As night fell, it started to get cold.

Karim pointed to a bright star. "That's Polaris," he said. "It tells us which way is north."

On and on they walked, worn out and shivering with cold.

"Look how low that star is," said Amira, pointing ahead.

Karim frowned. "That's not a star," he said.

When they got closer, they saw that the light was a campfire. Kneeling camels and sleeping Tuareg men rested close by.

The children whooped and punched the air.
"It's a salt caravan!" they shouted. "We're saved!"

"We come in peace!" said Karim in French.

"We're cold and tired," pleaded Amira. "Please help us."

The Tuaregs led them to the campfire. "We are travelling to Agadez," they said. "Come with us, if you like."

A boy called Tijani brought them a bowl of camel milk and three blankets. "Get some sleep," he said. "We leave at sunrise."

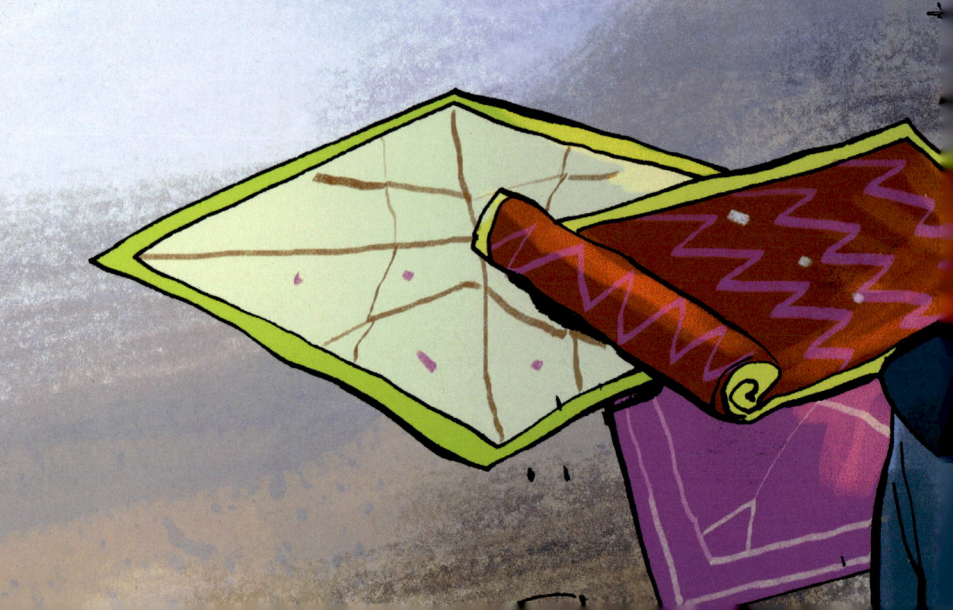

19

When Amira woke, the camels were ready to go. Each one carried four huge slabs of salt.

Amira stretched and reached for her shoes.

"Stop!" Tijani ran up, grabbed Amira's shoes and shook them upside-down. A yellow scorpion fell out onto the rug.

"First rule of the desert," laughed Tijani. "Always check your shoes before putting them on!"

After a delicious breakfast of dates and green tea, the caravan set off. Karim and Amira rode on one of the camels. Ali walked behind with Tijani.

At midday, they reached an oasis and stopped to let the camels drink. Ali, Amira and Tijani jumped into the cool water and splashed around.

The afternoon walk was very long and very hot, but at last they saw some red brick houses on the horizon.

"There's Agadez," cried Tijani.

Karim laughed and hugged his children. "Well done, both of you!" he said. "We may have lost a plane, but we've survived our Sahara adventure!"

Talk about the story

Answer the questions:

1 What were Karim's children called?

2 Where did the family live and where were they flying to?

3 What were the Tuareg's camels carrying through the desert?

4 Can you think of another word that means the same as 'trudged'? (page 15)

5 Why did Karim have to land the plane during the sandstorm?

6 How does Tijani save Amira on the morning after the plane crash?

7 What do you think will happen to the family when they arrive in Agadez?

8 Would you like to deliver planes? Do you think it would be a difficult job?

Can you retell the story in your own words?